queens
of
STEAM

Dr. Carla Hayden

The First Woman
Librarian of Congress

by Mari Bolte

Image credits: Cover: The Washington Post/Getty Images; 3: Leigh Vogel/ Getty Images; 4: Michael Kovak/Getty Images; 5: recebin/Shutterstock; 6: Zhukov Oleg/Shutterstock; 7: tovovan/Shutterstock; 8: Bettmann/Getty Images; 9: Adriana.Macias/Shutterstock; 10: Alena Divina/Shutterstock; 11: Hendrickson Photography/Shutterstock; 12: Jonathan Bachman/Getty Images; 15: Caroline Brehman/Getty Images; 16: Drew Angerer/Getty Images; 17: Vava Vladimir Jovanovic/Shutterstock; 18: Keystone Features/ Getty Images; 20: Sean Zanni/Getty Images; 21: Oomka/Shutterstock; 22: SeventyFour/Shutterstock; 23: Shannon Finney/Getty Images; 24: Pool/Getty Images; 25: Laura Reyero/Shutterstock; 26: HECTOR MATA/Getty Images; 27: Dia Dipasupil/Getty Images; 31: robuart/Shutterstock, ARIP YULIANTO/ Shutterstock; background: incomible/Getty Images

9781223187457 English Hardcover
9781223187464 English Paperback
9781223187471 English eBook

Published by Paw Prints Publishing
PawPrintsPublishing.com
Printed in China

See the Glossary on page 29 for definitions of words found in **bold** in the text!

"Please join me on a journey."

–Dr. Carla Hayden

Her Kingdom:

Libraries: Literacy and Learning

"Queen of **STEAM**" Dr. Carla Hayden
is a pioneer of library science.

Check Out This "Queen"

On September 14, 2016, a crowd gathers. They are at the Thomas Jefferson Building in Washington, D.C. History is about to be made.

Dr. Carla Hayden places her hand upon the Bible. Then, she takes an **oath** to become the Librarian of Congress. She is the first woman and the first Black person to hold that honor.

The Library of Congress is the biggest **public library** in the United States. It is made up of three separate buildings connected by an underground tunnel system!

Queens is part of New York City. It is made up of many distinct neighborhoods, each with its own culture and history. It is one of the most diverse urban areas in the world.

The Accidental Librarian

Dr. Carla was born on August 10, 1952, in Tallahassee, Florida. Both of her parents were musicians. Dr. Carla spent her early childhood in Queens, New York. Instead of reading music, Dr. Carla fell in love with reading books.

Dr. Carla was born the same year *Charlotte's Web* was published: 1952.

Growing up, Dr. Carla enjoyed reading books about royalty, among other things. Books on Henry VIII and Anne Boleyn, for example, often made Dr. Carla's reading list as a child.

Dr. Carla's parents divorced in 1962. Afterward, Dr. Carla moved with her mother to Illinois. She spent summers in the city of Springfield. Abraham Lincoln had lived there. Because of that, Dr. Carla felt a special connection to this historical figure.

Five Quick Facts about Dr. Carla Hayden

Eleanor Roosevelt

1. Favorite children's book: *Bright April* by Marguerite de Angeli

2. Favorite book genre: Cozy mysteries

3. Favorite female historical figure: Eleanor Roosevelt

4. Favorite bingeable TV: Home improvement shows

5. Favorite ice cream flavor: Chocolate

The Chicago Public Library was started in 1873. The city's previous libraries had all been private and cost money to access.

In 1973, Dr. Carla got a degree in political science from Chicago's Roosevelt University. Then, it was time for her to choose a path. Would she be a **social worker**? A lawyer? Both **careers** meant more school. More school meant she'd need a job to help pay her way.

A friend told her that the Chicago Public Library was hiring. Dr. Carla loved books and libraries. It couldn't hurt to apply! This first job as a children's services librarian would become a career. Dr. Carla has called herself an "accidental librarian."

Dr. Carla's first job with the library was at Chicago's South Side **branch**. It was inside a building where a store used to be. Dr. Carla saw how much the library helped the neighborhood. She realized the library and its **resources** helped make people's lives easier.

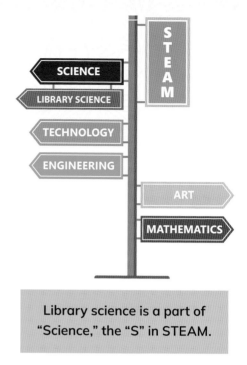

Library science is a part of "Science," the "S" in STEAM.

Then, Dr. Carla made a discovery that would change the rest of her life. One of her coworkers was working on an **advanced degree**. It was in library science. Dr. Carla hadn't even realized that was possible! She decided she wanted to do that, too.

Got late fees? Not anymore! In 2019, the Chicago Public Library stopped collecting late fees for overdue books. It was the largest public library in the United States to do this.

Visitors to the Chicago Museum of Science and Industry can explore an airplane, submarine, and spacecraft module.

In 1982, Dr. Carla changed jobs. For five years, she worked at Chicago's Museum of Science and Industry. Her job was to display the museum's **collections** of interesting and valuable objects for the public to see.

Then, Dr. Carla moved to Pennsylvania to work for the University of Pittsburgh. She taught at the School of Library and Information Science until 1991.

Dr. Carla talked to Michelle Obama about the former first lady's memoir *Becoming* at a 2018 conference for the American Library Association.

A Throne Made of Books

Dr. Carla returned to Chicago in 1991 to serve the people of the Windy City again. This time, it would be as deputy commissioner and chief librarian. Her role gave her reign over the city's entire library system! She did this for two years.

Dr. Carla met a lawyer named Michelle Robinson while in Chicago. Michelle had just started dating a young man named Barack. Later, this couple—who became President and First Lady Obama—would have a huge impact on Dr. Carla's life.

Enoch Pratt Free Library in Baltimore, Maryland, is one of the oldest free libraries in America. Dr. Carla was hired as its chief executive officer in 1993. She would bring the Baltimore library system into the digital age. More computers were added for library users. Resources and collections were **digitized**. Dr. Carla also added space for teens to gather and do their homework after school.

Pratt's Progress Report

Students aren't the only ones who get progress reports! The Enoch Pratt Library does a progress report each year. What grade would you give the library for this progress report?

- In 2021, the library set a goal. It wanted 20 percent more people to come to special programs by the end of 2022.
- By 2022, it was 93 percent of the way toward its goal.

Special Program Attendance

2021	73,246 people
2022	81,482 people
Goal	87,895 people

2022, Enoch Pratt Free Library

Dr. Carla is not afraid to speak out. She protested the 2001 Patriot Act. The law allowed the government to see what books people checked out at libraries. Dr. Carla thought this violated people's privacy.

During this time, Dr. Carla also served as president of the American Library Association (ALA) (2003–2004). The ALA supports librarians. It works to improve libraries. Dr. Carla ran on the idea of "**Equity** of Access." She believes that everyone, no matter their age or background, should have access to the information they need.

Dr. Carla remained a leader at Enoch Pratt Public Library. In 2015, a Black man named Freddie Gray was killed by Baltimore police. Demonstrations against **police brutality** took place around the country. Protests in Baltimore became violent. Many businesses and services in the city closed during the protests. Dr. Carla kept the library open because she thought there should be a safe space for people to go, especially with the nation in crisis.

That same year, the US Government **Accountability** Office wrote a report to Congress. It said the Library of Congress didn't have proper leadership. It also wasn't keeping up with technology. It needed a new leader who could bring the library into the modern age. President Barack Obama nominated Dr. Carla.

President Obama said Dr. Carla "has the proven experience, dedication, and deep knowledge of our nation's libraries to serve our country well."

A Brief History of Libraries

- 600s BCE*: The oldest known library is built in current-day Iraq.
- 200s BCE: The Library of Alexandria is founded in Egypt.
- 830 CE*: The House of Wisdom is founded in Baghdad.
- 1571: The Laurentian Library opens in Florence, Italy.
- 1731: Benjamin Franklin establishes the first lending library in America.
- 1800: The Library of Congress is founded.
- 1903: The first Carnegie Library opens to the public; millionaire Andrew Carnegie donated $60 million to fund 1,689 free public libraries across America.

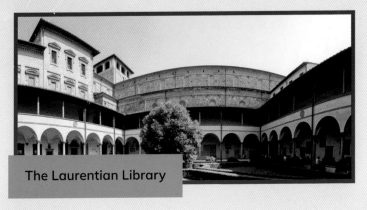

The Laurentian Library

*Before Common Era (BCE) is before year 1. Common Era (CE) is year 1 and after.

Dr. Carla calls librarians the "original search engines."
Children's librarians have been helping kids find information
since before computers, such as in the 1950s in New York City.

Libraries: Kingdoms of Knowledge

Librarians are educators, but they are also historians, researchers, and technology whizzes. Library science focuses on organizing, preserving, and using information. It also has the goal of helping people learn from what they find. Librarians don't know all the answers, but they know how to find out the answers!

Branch libraries are part of a main library system. For example, the Enoch Pratt Free Library is the main system. There is a large Central Library and headquarters in downtown Baltimore. There are 21 smaller branch libraries spread throughout the city. It's like a tree of libraries!

The Library of Congress is the ultimate place to learn. It holds more than 173 million items. And that number is always growing! The library gets two copies of each work published in the United States. Not just books. They also receive movies, audiobooks, maps, sheet music, and **artifacts**. Every day, around 10,000 new items are added.

The library was founded in 1800. It is full of rare books from around the world. One is a printing of a book called *Old King Cole*. It is one of the smallest books in the world. It measures around 1 millimeter tall. That's the length of a pencil tip!

Musician Lizzo visited with Dr. Hayden at the Library of Congress in 2022. She played a flute from its collection.

Librarians of Congress serve for 10 years. Most never served as a librarian before being **appointed** to the position. Many were writers, historians, businesspeople, or lawyers before taking the role.

The Library of Congress was founded to serve members of Congress. Anyone 16 years and older can visit the Library of Congress and read the books there. However, only government officials and library staff can check out materials.

How we create and use information changes all the time. Libraries must keep up with it all! In 2010, the Library of Congress started adding tweets to its collection. Hundreds of years from now, we'll be able to research and read the very first tweet on Twitter: "just setting up my twttr"!

We Need Libraries

- 1.5 billion people visit public libraries every year.
- Most libraries offer free internet.
- 70 percent of libraries are the only free computer and internet provider in their communities.
- 14,700 people participate in free library classes every day.
- In 2018, more than 2 billion books, eBooks, and other items were borrowed from libraries.

Each year, the Library of Congress awards a prize to a musician for their lifetime achievement. In 2022, Dr. Carla presented the award to soul musician Lionel Richie.

Thinking about the future of libraries is a test for any "Queen of STEAM." Librarians like Dr. Carla are true time travelers. They collect and preserve the past. But they also make sure their people are ready for the future. Dr. Carla had a big job ahead of her. Could she bring America's oldest library into the 21st century and beyond?

By attending important meetings and conferences, naming the nation's poet laureate, and overseeing the US Copyright Office, Dr. Carla plays an active role in supporting the modern American way of life.

Lady of the Library

Dr. Carla took on the challenge. Her first goal was to share the library's treasures. She would "throw open the treasure chest" to everyone. Dr. Carla vowed to make the first half of the library's collection digital within five years. And she did! Now, people around the world can visit the library and explore the collection from their home, using their computer.

The Library of Congress's digital collection can be viewed at www.loc.gov/collections. There are rare books, maps, photographs, music recordings, and more.

Have you ever wanted to learn how to make a TikTok dance? Dreamed of hearing an award-winning author read their work? Listen to an online concert? Or even make your own music? The Library of Congress has programs that make all that possible. You can even become a virtual volunteer.

Of the People: Widening the Path

Of the People: Widening the Path is a project that encourages people from underrepresented groups to add their unique stories to the Library of Congress collection. New videos, photos, books, and music are sought out to highlight cultural and community diversity and create a more inclusive collection at the library. America has a rich history. Recording all sides of that history is important. Check it out at www.loc.gov/programs/of-the-people!

Dr. Carla has said that the Library of Congress is "for people who are curious. People who want to create or learn."

As Librarian of Congress, Dr. Carla is interested in connecting with her fellow Americans. She is the first Librarian of Congress to tweet, and she's also active on Instagram. In 2022, she tweeted, "Libraries are safe havens and sanctuaries for ALL people." Dr. Carla's reign will last until 2026. But her time spent leading the Library of Congress will be celebrated for years to come.

Quiz

1. The Librarian of Congress serves a term of:
   A. forever
   B. 5 years
   C. 10 years
   D. 20 years

2. The Library of Congress adds _____ new pieces to its collection every day.
   A. 73,000
   B. 10,000
   C. 20,000
   D. 13,500

3. "Equity" means:
   A. recognizing that things are not always fair for everyone but working to correct that balance
   B. everyone gets the same thing
   C. the center of the earth
   D. quitting something new

4. People use libraries to:
   A. learn new things
   B. write reports
   C. see historical documents
   D. use computers
   E. all of the above

Glossary

accountability (uh-kount-uh-BIL-uh-tee): being held responsible for actions

advanced degree (ad-VANST duh-GREE): a college degree beyond the undergraduate level; a master's degree and doctorate are advanced degrees

appointed (uh-POYN-tehd): when a person is assigned to an important job

artifacts (AR-tuh-fakts): objects that were made by people in the past

branch (BRANCH): a separate part of a central organization

careers (kuh-REERS): jobs that people have that they stay in for a long time

collections (kuh-LEK-shuhns): groups of objects that have been brought together

digitized (DIH-juh-tized): has been converted into a digital form so it can be viewed on a computer; pictures, text, and sound can be digitized

equity (EHK-wuh-tee): treating people with fairness and justice

oath (OHTH): a solemn promise, often given in front of witnesses

police brutality (puh-LEES broo-TAL-uh-tee): excessive use of force used on someone by law enforcement

public library (PUH-blik LAI-brehr-ee): a library that the general public can use for free

resources (REE-sor-suhz): a supply of materials available to use

social worker (SOH-shuhl WUR-ker): a person who works to help people who are having problems

STEAM (STEEM): the fields of Science, Technology, Engineering, Arts, and Mathematics; library science is a part of science

Check in at the Library

Your local library depends on patrons like you! Every time someone visits, checks out a book in person or online, uses a collection, or attends a program, it shows how important the library is to the community. Libraries provide clean, safe places for everyone. It's time to pay yours a visit! There's so much more to do than just browse the aisles. Grab your favorite adult and ask them for a lift to the library.

- With an adult's help, get a library card or create an online account.
- Check out a book or an eBook.
- Participate in a library program, such as an art class, book club, or after-school group. Find out when the next author visit is, or attend a discussion panel.
- Volunteer your time. Maybe you will be shelving books, selling used books, or tidying up workspaces. This is a great activity to do with family and friends.
- Meet the people who work in the library and find out more about what they do. How did they get to where they are? Do they have any advice for you?

ACTIVITY

Thank a Librarian

Librarians have a lot of important work to do! Let them know you appreciate them and that their contributions aren't going unnoticed. Everyone likes knowing that they are doing a good job. Take a minute out of your day and drop a word of encouragement.

- Write a letter to a librarian to thank them for their contribution to the community. Send it as a card in the mail or as an email to everyone.
- Do you have a favorite exhibit, section, or activity at the library? Let them know! What did you like about it?
- Share special stories or memories about the library. What was the first book you checked out? Do you remember your very first visit?
- If there's something you think the library should change, write that, too. Your opinion matters!

Index

Chicago Public Library, 9, 10

Chicago's Museum of Science and Industry, 11

digital, 14, 25

Enoch Pratt Free Library, 14, 16, 19

library collections, 11, 14, 20, 22, 25–26

Library of Congress, 5, 16–17, 20–23, 25–27

library visits, 20–22, 25

Obama, Barack and Michelle, 12–13, 16

technology, 16, 19

University of Pittsburgh, 11

virtual libraries, 26